On a tree-lined street in Boston,
in an old mansion,

at the top of the stairs,

in a second-floor room,

empty frames hang,

waiting. . . .

Neal Porter Books

Text copyright © 2021 by Candace Fleming
Illustrations copyright © 2021 by Matthew Cordell
All Rights Reserved
HOLIDAY HOUSE is registered in the U.S. Patent and Trademark Office.
Printed and bound in April 2021 at Toppan Leefung, DongGuan City, China.
The artwork for this book was created using pen and ink (Hero 9018 fountain pen
with Noodler's Black) and watercolor on Canson cold press watercolor paper.
www.holidayhouse.com
First Edition
1 3 5 7 9 10 8 6 4 2
Library of Congress Cataloging-in-Publication Data

Names: Fleming, Candace, author. | Cordell, Matthew, 1975– illustrator.
Title: What Isabella wanted / by Candace Fleming ; illustrated by
Matthew Cordell.
Description: First edition. | New York : Holiday House, [2021] | "A Neal
Porter Book." | Includes bibliographical references. | Audience: Ages 4
to 8 | Audience: Grades K–1 | Summary: "The true story of Isabella
Stewart Gardner's mission to turn her home into a unique art museum"
— Provided by publisher.
Identifiers: LCCN 2020044131 | ISBN 9780823442638 (hardcover)
Subjects: LCSH: Gardner, Isabella Stewart, 1840-1924—Juvenile literature.
| Isabella Stewart Gardner Museum—Juvenile literature.
Classification: LCC N5220.G26 F59 2021 | DDC 708.744/61—dc23
LC record available at https://lccn.loc.gov/2020044131

ISBN 978-0-8234-4263-8 (hardcover)

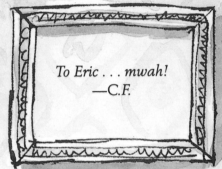

*In loving memory of
Professor Paul Martyka,
who gave me and so many
others the gifts of art, a
critical eye, and individual
expression* —M.C.

To Eric . . . mwah!
—C.F.

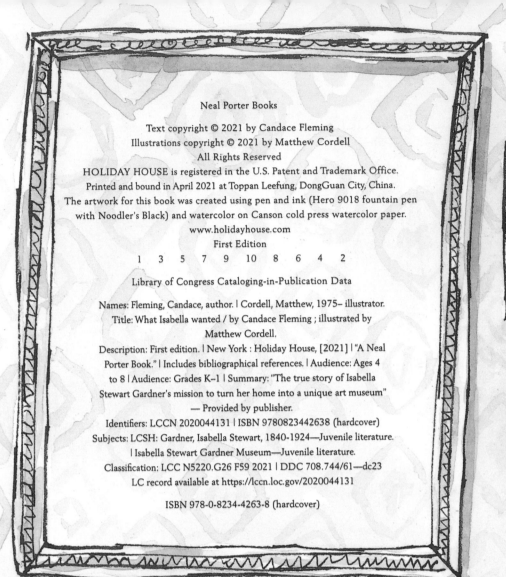

What Isabella Wanted

Isabella Stewart Gardner Builds a Museum

Candace Fleming

Illustrated by Matthew Cordell

NEAL PORTER BOOKS

HOLIDAY HOUSE / NEW YORK

It all begin with Isabella—

brash,

extravagant

Isabella—

who wore baseball gear
to the symphony,

and greeted her guests
perched in a potted palm tree,

and strolled zoo lions up Beacon Street,
and outraged all society,

exactly as Isabella wanted.

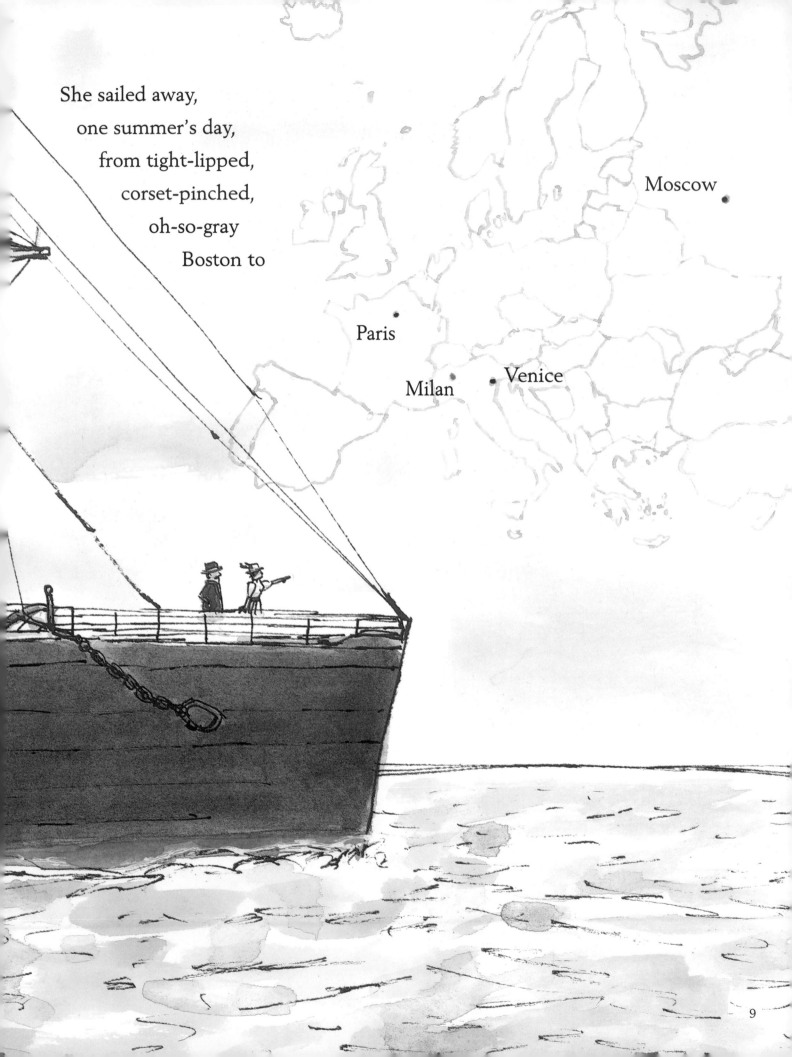

She sailed away,
  one summer's day,
    from tight-lipped,
    corset-pinched,
    oh-so-gray
      Boston to

Moscow

Paris

Milan   Venice

seeking adventure,

and finding it in art,

in galleries, and gardens, and great estates,

on every wall,

in every space,

heart-soaring, mind-seizing, world-shifting

Art!

Truth and beauty.
Otherworldly.

In a Venice courtyard, she flung her arms wide.

Art!

It was suddenly
exactly what Isabella wanted.

Landscapes,

seascapes,

portraits
of saints,

stained
glass,

tapestries,

Roman mosaics,

medieval tables,

Renaissance chairs, and—

Oh!

Vermeer's *The Concert,*

and—

Oh!

Rembrandt's *The Storm,*

and more,

so much more,
always more,
exactly as Isabella wanted,
filling her Beacon Street mansion,

every
wall,
every
space.

Outside, Boston's gray rain puddled the snow,
but inside she gazed at *The Concert*,
sat for long hours in front of *The Storm*,
thinking and dreaming,
happy and warm.

While far away in Asia and Europe,
art buyers roamed ancient cities,
ferreting out paintings,
tracking down sculptures,
sniffing out Old World treasures,
all for Isabella.

Will you buy a rare
Persian rug?
I WANT IT!

A peerless terra-cotta
sculpture?
GRAB IT!

A real, unquestionable,
perfect Raphael?
SOLD!

Her agents did as they were told,
then shipped the objects to Boston,
hiding them,
disguising them,
smuggling them out of
Italy,
Egypt,
Japan,

breaking the law,
but doing,
exactly as Isabella wanted.

Her ambitions grew with her collection.
Now, she imagined . . .
a museum in a home,
filled with her paintings,
her statues,
her objects of art—

a home in a museum, filled with her scrapbooks, her letters,
her travel souvenirs, all precious items, displayed side by side,
for people to come and enjoy.

"It's my pleasure," declared Isabella.
Her vision. Her will.

Every decision—choosing the land, drawing up plans, hiring the workers—
was hers.

And every day at the worksite she clambered up ladders,
scurried across scaffolding, hacked at beams,
plastered walls, supervised, complained,
gave orders to . . .

do and redo, set and reset,
brick and rebrick, build and rebuild
an Italian palazzo that rose up
on that empty swampland—
the Fens—
with courtyard,
and cloisters,
and intimate rooms,

exactly as Isabella wanted.

She moved into the top floor,
but saved the other three for her glories.
She arranged them herself, each piece,
big and small, for more than a year,
with passion and flair,

pondering,
puzzling,
the placement of every object,

in every room,
on every wall,
in every space.

Where to put
that lock of poet's hair?
Where to place
those gilded chairs?

Isabella experimented.
She mixed and matched.

And in a second-floor room, she slipped *The Concert*
into a carved wooden frame near the window.

She placed *The Storm* in a gilded frame on the wall.

At last, she flung her arms wide.
Every last detail was . . .

. . . *exactly* as Isabella wanted.

New Years Day, 1903. The grand opening.

Visitors circled around her courtyard,
and through her second- and third-floor rooms,

feasting on
champagne,
doughnuts,
and art—
so much art—
on every wall,
in every space,

visitors lingering,
returning,
wandering around and
among her objects in awe.

Isabella followed after them,
shouting,
"Don't touch! Don't touch!"

Didn't they know that everything
was carefully arranged,
exactly as Isabella wanted?

Twenty days a year,
for more than twenty years,
Isabella opened the doors
of her museum home
to everyone, from art lovers
to street car conductors.
And when the doors closed . . .

she added more art, she filled
every room, she arranged and
rearranged her work in
progress, an extension of
herself, a gift she left
at the end of her long life,
to the people of Boston . . .

to keep forever,
just as long as *nothing*
was moved.
Not a cup.
Not a cross.
Not a painting.
Not a thing.

And that is how her
museum home stayed.
For decades.
Untouched.
Unchanged.
Exactly as Isabella wanted.

Until...

. . . under cover of darkness,
two thieves in disguise
broke into Isabella's museum home.
Art!
Art everywhere!

They grabbed,

and snatched,

and on the second floor
they cut away *The Concert*.

They cut away *The Storm*.

Then thieves and treasures disappeared
into the night.

Where did they go?

No one knows.

The police searched.

The FBI searched.

Private detectives searched.

They are still searching.

And on the second floor, empty frames enclose nothing but green brocade wall.

The Concert, *The Storm*, and other works—gone.

And so the place waits, longingly,

for the day her glories are returned,

and her museum home once more

will be complete,

unchanged,

exactly as Isabella wanted.

Isabella Stewart Gardner
1840–1924
"It's my pleasure"

This was Isabella Stewart Gardner's motto. The words, written in French—"C'est mon plaisir"—are even carved above the entryway to the Italian-style palazzo she built and filled with art. This grand old house on the Fenway in Boston, now called the Isabella Stewart Gardner Museum, uniquely reflects Isabella's eccentric personality. Designed not just as a place to house art, it was also her home from 1901 until her death in 1924. There she lived among the objects of her collection.

Some of these objects are works of art, but others are things she gathered and used during her life—letters and journals, dishes and teacups, dried leaves and seashells. All are given equal value, great art displayed next to bric-a-brac with no distinction between them. Additionally, the arrangement of each room is based entirely on Isabella's taste. Objects are not organized historically, or by artistic styles. They are definitely not meant to educate. Rather, they are all about Isabella and *her* connections to and feelings toward the art. She wanted visiting her collection to evoke pleasure, to affect those who saw it the way she was affected. She believed that art is an important part of what makes life worthwhile, and that art and everyday life are inseparable.

This is why she left her museum to the people of Boston forever, just as long as none of her arrangements are touched. She wanted *her* sense of our relationship with art to be the only focus.

Isabella Stewart Gardner
John Singer Sargent, 1888
Isabella Stewart Gardner Museum, Boston, MA,
USA/Bridgeman Images

(Rembrandt's *Christ in the Storm on the Sea of Galilee)*. Isabella often bought these masterpieces sight unseen.

Isabella definitely broke the rules in her zeal for art. She collected in a time when rich Americans were literally taking apart crumbling villas, purchased from owners no longer able to afford them, and shipping them home. They were buying up masterpieces from churches and temples. Authorities across Europe and Asia began cracking down on this wholesale looting of their countries' treasures. To get around these laws, Isabella urged her art buyers to create fake bills of sale, or smuggle objects

And Isabella Stewart Gardner *always* got what she wanted. The wife of a Boston millionaire, she enjoyed being flamboyant, and flung herself into anything that smacked of adventure. She raced cars, gambled on horses at the track, and once staged a boxing match in her drawing room. While the men fought, Isabella danced. Her behavior shocked Boston's stuffy society. But Isabella enjoyed this too. She loved breaking the rules.

It was on a trip to Europe in 1867 that Isabella was bitten with what she called "the picture habit." She decided to spend all her money on art. Her first major purchase was Vermeer's *The Concert*, which she bought in 1891 after seeing it in a Paris auction house. Most of her art, however, was purchased with the help of art advisers who lived in Europe and Asia. They recommended hundreds of the masterpieces in her museum, including *The Storm*

out in false-bottomed trucks. Isabella saw this as saving the art. Nowadays, we would call it cultural raiding. And we would call Isabella a thief.

Isabella began building her palazzo in 1899, taking two and a half years to complete it. It took her another year to install her collection. The place she called Fenway Court— it was renamed the Isabella Stewart Gardner Museum after her death—was open to the public just twenty days a year. On those days, everyone who could afford the dollar admittance fee was welcome. But almost immediately after its grand opening in 1903, some of her small treasures began disappearing. Isabella had no choice but to hire guards. Isabella herself walked around the galleries, shouting at visitors, "Don't touch!" over and over again.

Surprisingly, the collection remained mostly intact until the early morning hours of March 18, 1990, when two thieves disguised as policemen made off with an estimated $500 million in art from Isabella's collection—thirteen works altogether. None of it has been recovered, and the theft remains one of America's most enduring crime mysteries.

The empty frames still hang in the museum, which is offering a $10 million reward for information leading to the stolen works' return.

Want to visit Isabella's museum? You can, either in person or by going to www.gardnermuseum.org. Once there, you can meander through her collection—room to room and floor to floor—from her always-blooming indoor Courtyard with its ancient Roman sculpture garden, to her churchlike third-floor Gothic Room, where a life-sized portrait of Isabella herself gazes out from a dark corner.

Be sure to stop in the second-floor Dutch Room and pause before those sad, empty frames. And peek into the Titian Room where Isabella displayed a piece of her own white silk designer gown just below a world-renowned masterpiece. Yes, it's all a glorious jumble, a mishmash of art and architecture. It's strange and disorienting, contradictory and repetitious and . . . exactly what Isabella wanted.

BIBLIOGRAPHY

Boser, Ulrich. *The Gardner Heist: The True Story of the World's Largest Unsolved Art Theft*. New York: Harper Paperbacks, 2010.

Goldfarb, Hilliard T. *The Isabella Stewart Gardner Museum: A Companion Guide and History*. New Haven, CT: Yale University Press, 1995.

Hawley, Anne, Robert Campbell, and Alexander Wood. *Isabella Stewart Gardner: Daring by Design*. New York: Skira Rizzoli, 2014.

Lucey, Donna M. *Sargent's Women: Four Lives Behind the Canvas*. New York: W.W. Norton, 2017.

Shand-Tucci, Douglass. *The Art of Scandal: The Life and Times of Isabella Stewart Gardner*. New York: HarperCollins, 1998.

Tharp, Louise Hall. *Mrs. Jack: A Biography of Isabella Stewart Gardner*. New York: Peter Weed Books, 1984.

Vigderman, Patricia. *The Memory Palace of Isabella Stewart Gardner*. Tucson, AZ: Hol Art Books, 2014, EPUB.

SOURCE NOTES

19: "It's my pleasure": https://www.gardnermuseum.org/experience/collection/15079.

29: "Don't touch!": Lucey, 238.

39: "the picture habit": Lucey, 220.